The Story of a Special Day
Volume 35

February

4

The 35th day of the year. There are 330 days (331 in leap years) remaining until the end of the year.

by Michael Dobson

Timespinner
Press

This book is also available in e-book form for Kindle, e-pub devices, and other formats from your favorite online booksellers.

For more information about the series, about us, or about your special day, please email us at editor@timespinnerpress.com.

Look for other volumes in *The Story of a Special Day*, coming often. See www.timespinnerpress.com for details and for the most recent information.

Table of Contents

Cover: Portrait of George Washington by Thomas Sully (Courtesy LBJ Museum). Washington was elected president on February 4, 1789 — the EVENT OF THE DAY.

Quote of the Day

"What kind of man would live where there is no danger? I don't believe in taking foolish chances. But nothing can be accomplished by not taking a chance at all."

Charles Lindbergh, aviator
born February 4, 1902

Today in History

February 4

The 1789 inaguration of first US President George Washington

Event of the Day
George Washington Elected President of the United States

On February 4, 1789, George Washington was elected the first President of the United States by unanimous vote of the Electoral College.

War and Peace

While major combat in the American Revolutionary War ended with the surrender of General Cornwallis at Yorktown on October 19, 1781, official hostilities continued until the signing of the Treaty of Paris, in which Great Britain recognized the independence of the United States, on September 3, 1783.

It was a time of great tension. Continental Army soldiers, who hadn't been paid, grew restless and there were several attempted mutinies, until the Continental Congress was able to scrape together a bonus. Upon signing of the treaty, the United States elected not to have a standing army, and Washington disbanded his forces with an eloquent farewell address given on November 2, 1783. He resigned as commander-in-chief the following month, returning to his home at Mount Vernon in the hopes of retiring into private life. This, however, was not to be the case.

Washington, an advocate of a strong Federal government and an opponent of the weak Articles of Confederation, was persuaded to attend the Constitutional Convention in Philadelphia in 1787, and was promptly elected president of the Convention, where he supported the development of the new Constitution, though he declined to vote for his ratification on the grounds that he already expected to be a candidate for President.

The Electoral College

Under the new constitution, ordinary citizens did not vote directly for either senators or the Presidency. While the House of Representatives was supposed to be the "people's house," directly elected by the citizens, Senators represented the states, and so were elected by state legislatures.

The Constitutional Convention contemplated different methods of electing the President. Election by Congress was thought to compromise presidential independence. Direct election was rejected because while northern states had wide suffrage (right to vote), southern states restricted the vote, especially where slaves were concerned.

As a compromise, the selection of the President was delegated to an Electoral College, with members chosen however each state decided. In some states, voters elected their Electoral College representatives directly, while others left the decision to their state legislatures. Electoral College members were supposed to be independent, but soon each state adopted a "winner take all" system, in which electors pledged to vote for a certain candidate would all be chosen together. It wasn't until after the Civil War that states chose their electors by popular vote.

Although in most US states, the name of the presidential candidate appears on the ballot, voters are not actually voting for that person, but rather for a slate of electors pledged to that person.

Washington's Election

For the first Presidential election, each state legislature chose its electors, and on February 4, 1789, each state's electors met in their respective state capitol to cast their votes. Washington, the only presidential candidate in US history not affiliated with a political party, was elected unanimously (and would be elected unanimously again for a second term in 1792). No other US president has ever been elected unanimously, although James Monroe (who ran opposed in 1820) received all but a single vote.

Because it took some time for ballots to reach Philadelphia (then the capital of the United States), the inauguration of Washington did not take place until April 30, 1789. For the oath ceremony, Washington borrowed a robe worn by the British monarch in his annual address to Parliament, and following his swearing-in, gave a brief speech. Following the speech, Washington arranged for Barbados rum to be served to his guests.

Washington's Presidency

As the first president, Washington established many of the policies and norms associated with that office. He nominated the first judges for the Supreme Court, established a Cabinet consisting of consultants, supporters, and the heads of the newly created Federal departments. He created the roles of Secretary of State, Secretary of the Treasury, Secretary of War, and Postmaster-General.

As President, Washington played a leading role in the development of a new Federal capital in Washington, DC, although the years of his presidency were primarily spent in Philadelphia and New York City. He faced major challenges in the Northwest Indian War and the Whisky Rebellion. With his Treasury secretary, Alexander Hamilton, he established the First Bank of the United States and the US Mint to help repair the dire financial condition of the new nation.

Washington was reelected in 1792, but refused to run for a third term. His Farewell Address, published September 19, 1796, was an open letter to the people, is considered a classic statement of republican values.

Washington himself retired to his home in Mount Vernon, until his death on December 14, 1799. He is widely considered one of the three greatest presidents in American history, alongside Abraham Lincoln and Franklin Delano Roosevelt. Following his death, he was eulogized as "first in war, first in peace, and first in the hearts of his countrymen."

George Washington on Mount Rushmore

Image from *The 47 Ronin* (1941)

What Happened on February 4?

From the creation of great works of engineering and art, to devastating wars and natural disasters, thousands of years of history have left their mark on each and every day of the year. Here are some important events that occurred on February 4. (Items with a photo or illustration are boxed.)

1703 — In one of the most famous episodes in Japanese history, a group of **forty-seven Rōnin** (四十七士), or leaderless samurai, avenge the death of their *daimyo* (feudal lord) by killing the man responsible, and then commit *seppuku* (切腹), or ritual suicide for the murder they committed. The story has been told in plays, films, and books, and remains a hugely popular story in Japan.

1794 — The French First Republic **abolishes slavery** in all its territories (although Napoléon reestablishes it in 1802).

1846 — A group of **Mormon pioneers** under the direction of Brigham Young **head west** from Nauvoo, Illinois, eventually arriving in the Salt Lake Valley.

1861 — Delegates from six US states meet in Montgomery, Alabama, and form the **Confederate States of America**.

1941 — The United Service Organization (**USO**) is founded to provide services and entertainment to US service members and their families.

1945 — Toward the end of World War II, the **Yalta Conference**, a meeting of the heads of government of the United States, the United Kingdom, and the Soviet Union, begins in the Crimean resort town of Yalta, to discuss the post-war reorganization of Europe.

1974 — The **Symbionese Liberation Army**, a US revolutionary organization, **kidnaps heiress Patty Hearst**.

2004 — The social networking site **Facebook** is founded.

(seated, from left to right) Winston Churchill, Franklin D. Roosevelt, and Joseph Stalin at the Yalta conference. (Courtesy National Museum of the US Navy)

Quote of the Day

"Time is the most precious gift in our possession, for it is the most irrevocable. This is what makes it so disturbing to look back upon the time which we have lost. Time lost is time when we have not lived a full human life, time unenriched by experience, creative endeavor, enjoyment, and suffering. Time lost is time not filled, time left empty."

Dietrich Bonhoeffer, theologian
born February 4, 1906

Births
and
Deaths

THERIACA
MAGNA

February 4

Charles Lindbergh, born February 4, 1902

Notable February 4 People

With the current world population at about seven billion people, on average about 19 million people also celebrate their birthdays on February 4 — and that isn't counting the millions and millions who came before! No matter when you were born, you share your birthday with many special people whose accomplishments (and occasionally embarrassments) have been noted as part of history.

In this section, you'll meet fascinating people who share your birthday. They're organized by what they're famous for, and then in reverse chronological order from most recent to earliest. Those who are shown in photographs or artwork have a box around them. We don't have photos of everyone, so please forgive us if your favorite person is missing.

Some of these people you've heard of, others may be new to you, but they all make up an important part of the reason that February 4 is a truly special day!

Wanda Rutkiewicz

Who Was Born on February 4?

Adventure

Wanda Rutkiewicz, mountaineer known as the first woman to make a successful climb of K2. *(1943)*

Charles Lindbergh, pioneering aviator best known for his solo non-stop flight from New York to Paris in 1927, and for the kidnapping of his son in 1932. *(1902) (Photo page 12.)*

Government, Politics, and Law

Evan Wolfson, attorney and activist named by Time as one of the 100 Most Influential People in the World for his leadership of the same-sex marriage movement. *(1957)*

Dan Quayle, US vice-president during the administration of George H. W. Bush. *(1947)*

Isabel Perón, first female president of any country in the world, served as president of Argentina from 1974 to 1976 following the death of her husband Juan Perón. *(1931)*

Rosa Parks, African-American seamstress who famously refused to give up her seat to a white man on a Montgomery, Alabama, bus, resulting in the Montgomery Bus Boycott, a key moment in modern civil rights history. *(1913) (Photo page 34.)*

Ludwig Erhard, postwar German economic minister and chancellor whose economic programs led to the *Wirtschaftswunder,* or economic miracle, referring to the rapid recovery of industry following the war. *(1897)*

Literature and Journalism

Ted White, Hugo Award winning American science fiction author and editor, music critic, performer, and radio host (as "Dr. Progresso"), best known as editor of *Amazing Stories* and *Heavy Medal. (1938)*

Russell Hoban, author best known for the award-winning *Riddley Walker,* along with numerous children's books. *(1925)*

Betty Friedan, author of the pioneering 1963 feminist work *The Feminine Mystique*, founded the National Organization for Women. *(1921*)*

Mackinley Kantor, novelist who won the Pulitzer Prize for his 1955 novel *Andersonville. (1904)*

Édouard Estaunié, French novelist trained as a scientist and engineer, created the word "telecommunications." *(1862)*

---

* Betty Friedan was born and died on the same day: February 4, 1921, to February 4, 2006.

Alice Cooper (Photo: Biha, CC BY-SA 4.0)

Music

Gavin DeGraw, singer-songwriter whose single "I Don't Want to Be" became the theme song for the television series *One Tree Hill. (1977)*

Natalie Imbruglia, Australian singer-songwriter who sold over 7 million copies of her 1997 album *Left of Middle;* appeared in films such as *Johnny English* and *Closed for Winter. (1975)*

Clint Black, country music singer-songwriter best known for his breakthrough hits "A Better Man" and "Killin' Time." *(1962)*

Clint Black poster (Photo: Dwight McCann/Chumash Casino Resort, CC BY-SA 2.5)

Kitarō (喜多郎), Japanese recording artist who won a Grammy for the 1999 new-age album *Thinking of You.* (1953)

Alice Cooper, singer-songwriter known as "the godfather of shock rock," whose best known hit was the 1972 single "School's Out." *(1948) (Photo previous page.)*

Performing Arts

Gabrielle Anwar, actress known for her tango with Al Pacino in the 1992 film *Scent of a Woman,* and for her co-starring role in the 2007-2013 television series *Burn Notice. (1970)*

Jonathan Larson, composer and playwright who received three Tony Awards and a Pulitzer Prize for the rock musical *Rent. (1960)*

Adrienne King, actress best known for her portrayal of Alice Hardy in the *Friday the 13th* film franchise. *(1955)*

George Romero, filmmaker best known for his films about a zombie apocalypse, beginning with 1968's *Night of the Living Dead. (1940)*

David Brenner, stand-up comedian notable as one of the most frequent guests on *The Tonight Show Starring Johnny Carson. (1936)*

Ida Lupino

Conrad Bain, actor best known for his role as the father in the long-running sitcom *Diff'rent Strokes.* *(1923)*

Janet Waldo, voice artist best known as Judy Jetson from *The Jetsons* animated series. *(1920)*

Ida Lupino, actress known for such films as *High Sierra;* only woman in the Hollywood studio system era to become a director and producer in her own right. *(1918)*

Sir Norman Wisdom, English actor and comedian best known for a series of films featuring his character Norman Pitkin. *(1915)*

William Talman, actor best remembered as District Attorney Hamilton Burger in the television series *Perry Mason. (1915)*

Nigel Bruce, British character actor best known for his portrayal of Dr. Watson in the *Sherlock Holmes* film series starring Basic Rathbone. *(1895)*

Religion

Dietrich Bonhoeffer, German Lutheran pastor and theologian known for his anti-Nazi positions, executed by the Nazis toward the end of the war. *(1906)*

Science

Lotfi Zadeh, computer scientist and mathematician best known for the creation of partial set theory, commonly known as "fuzzy logic." *(1921)*

Clyde Tombaugh, American astronomer known for the discovery of Pluto. *(1906)*

Sports

Carlie Patterson, gymnast who won a gold medal as best all-around gymnast in the 2004 Olympics, member of the USA Gymnastics Hall of Fame. *(1988)*

Lucie Šafářová, Czech tennis player ranked as high as #4 worldwide. *(1987)*

Oscar De La Hoya, boxer who won ten world titles in six different weight classes, as well as an Olympic gold medal in the sport. *(1973)*

Denis Savard, ice hockey player named to the Hockey Hall of Fame in 2000. *(1961)*

Lawrence Taylor, linebacker for the New York Giants, named to the Pro Football Hall of Fame. *(1959)*

Dave Sands, Australian boxer inducted into the World Boxing Hall of Fame in 1998. *(1926)*

Gyula Grosics, Hungarian football (soccer) player considered one of the greatest goalkeepers of all time. *(1926)*

Byron Nelson, American golfer, member of the World Golf Hall of Fame. *(1912)*

Eddie Cochems, American football player and coach known as the "father of the forward pass." *(1877)*

Clyde Tombaugh

Lisa Fonssagrives (Photo: Toni Frissell)

Who Died on February 4?

Art and Illustration

Patrick Nagel, artist known for his art deco-influenced illustrations of women. *(1984)*

Illustration by Patrick Nagel (© Patrick Nagel)

Fashion and Modeling

Koos Van Den Akker, Dutch fashion designer known for creating the distinctive sweaters worn by Bill Cosby on *The Cosby Show. (2015)*

Lisa Fonssagrives, Swedish fashion model generally considered to be the first "supermodel." *(1992)*

Government and Military

Edgar Mitchell, piloted the lunar module for the Apollo 14 mission, sixth person to walk on the surface of the Moon. *(2016)*

Florence Green, served in the Women's Royal Air Force during World War I and was the last surviving veteran of that war from any country. *(2012)*

Carl Albert, Oklahoma congressman and Speaker of the US House of Representatives. *(2000)*

Literature and Journalism

Betty Friedan, see "Who Was Born February 4?"

Patricia Highsmith, author best known for the novel *Strangers on a Train*, which became a 1951 Hitchcock film, and *The Talented Mr. Ripley*, which became a 1999 film of the same name. *(1995)*

Neal Cassady, author and poet during the Beat era, model for the character Dean Moriarty in Jack Kerouac's novel *On the Road. (1968)*

Henry Kuttner, influential author of science fiction and fantasy under his own name and as "Lewis Padgett," whose most famous works include "Mimsy Were the Borogoves," adapted into a 2007 film *The Last Mimzy. (1958)*

Crew of the Apollo 14 mission. From left to right: Stuart A Roosa, Alan B. Shepard Jr., and **Edgar Mitchell** (Courtesy NASA)

Music

Maurice White, singer-songwriter who founded the band Earth, Wind, and Fire, member of the Rock and Roll Hall of Fame and the Songwriters Hall of Fame. *(2016)*

Reg Presley, lead singer for The Troggs, whose famous hits include "Wild Thing. and "With a Girl Like You." *(2013)*

Lux Interior, singer and member of the band The Cramps. *(2009)*

J. J. Johnson, jazz trombonist and composer of the bebop era. *(2001)*

Liberace, pianist and entertainer often called "Mr. Showmanship," known for his flamboyant costumes. *(1987)*

Karen Carpenter, singer and drummer for The Carpenters, hits included "We've Only Just Begun" and "Close to You," died of anorexia. *(1983)*

Louis Jordan, African-Amerian musician and songwriter known as the "King of the Jukebox," whose hits include "Choo Choo Ch'Boogie" and "Is You Is or Is You Ain't My Baby?" *(1975)*

Adolphe Sax, Belgian musician and inventor who developed the saxophone and other saxhorn instruments. *(1894)*

Performing Arts

Augusta Dabney, daytime drama actress best known for her role as Isabelle Alden on the soap opera *Loving.* *(2008)*

Ossie Davis, African-American actor, playwright, and civil rights activist known for his partnership/ marriage with Ruby Dee, awarded the National Medal of Arts. *(2005)*

Religion

John Rogers, Bible translator and editor, first English Protestant burned at the stake during the reign of English Queen Mary I ("Bloody Mary"). *(1558)*

Liberace (Photo: Allan Warren, CC BY-SA 3.0)

Science and Medicine

Carl Rogers, founding father of psychotherapy research who helped develop the humanistic approach to psychology. *(1987)*

Satyendra Nath Bose (সত্যেন্দ্রনাথ বসু), Bengali physicist important in the development of quantum mechanics, partnered with Albert Einstein to develop Bose-Einstein statistics and the theory of the Bose-Einstein condensate. The subatomic particles known as "bosons" are named for him. *(1974)*

Hendrik Lorentz, Dutch physicist who shared the 1902 Nobel Prize in Physics; developed the transformation equations that formed the basis of Einstein's theory of special relativity. *(1928)*

"February in the Isle of Wight," John Brett (1866)

Quote of the Day

"People always say that I didn't give up my seat because I was tired, but that isn't true. I was not tired physically, or no more tired than I usually was at the end of a working day. I was not old, although some people have an image of me as being old then. I was forty-two. No, the only tired I was, was tired of giving in."

Rosa Parks, seamstress and civil rights activist, born February 4, 1913

Holidays
Around
the World

February 4

Rosa Parks in 1955, with Dr. Martin Luther King, Jr., in the background. (National Archives) — for ROSA PARKS DAY

Holidays Around the World

If you're looking for a reason to take your special day off, you should know that every single day is a holiday somewhere in the world! Here's some of what you can celebrate on February 4!

General Events

Day of the Armed Struggle (Angola)

The Day of the Armed Struggle in the southwestern African nation of Anglo commemorates the Baixa de Cassanje revolt, which began tAngolan War of Independence.

Independence Day (Sri Lanka)

Many nations celebrate an Independence Day. The nation of Sri Lanka commemorates its internal political independence from British rule on February 4, 1948.

Rosa Parks Day (California, Missouri)

Rosa Parks Day is an official observance in four US states. In California and Missouri, it takes place on February 4, the birthday of Rosa Parks, and in Ohio and Oregon it takes place on December 1, the date of her arrest.

World Cancer Day (international)

World Cancer Day was founded by the Union for International Cancer Control, to combat misinformation, spread awareness, and encourage prevention and early detection of cancer.

Food Holidays

In the United States, almost every day of the year is dedicated to a particular food. (Some other countries also have official food days, but only in America is there one every single day!) Sponsored by manufacturers, retailers, farmers, or simply fans, these days are often proclaimed by the President, Congress, state governors, or mayors. Given that there are more different foods than days of the year, some days honor more than one kind of food!

In the US, February 4 is **National Homemade Soup Day.** The word "soup," according to Foodimentary, comes from a Middle English word *soupen*, "to drink in sips." It's also **National Stuffed Mushroom Day.** It's claimed that stuffed mushrooms, along with other kinds of finger food, became popular in the US during Prohibition, as people needed to find something to serve at parties in the absence of booze.

In addition, the entire month of February is used to celebrate numerous foods. Here's a list of what to eat in the month of February!

- Canned Food Month
- National Chocolate Lovers Month
- National Cherry Month
- National Grapefruit Month
- National Snack Food Month
- National Potato Lovers Month

- Return Shopping Carts to the Supermarket Month

- National Hot Breakfast Month

An abandoned shopping cart, by Michiel1972 (CC BY-SA 3.0) for RETURN SHOPPING CARTS TO THE SUPERMARKET MONTH

Religious Feast Days and Holidays

Mardi Gras (Shrove Tuesday)

French for "Fat Tuesday," this celebration takes place the day before Ash Wednesday, the beginning of the Lenten season. The New Orleans Mardi Gras celebration is perhaps the most famous, but Mardi Gras and the Carnival season (between Ephiphany and Ash Wednesday) are celebrated in many areas with large Catholic populations. It's known as *Karneval* or *Fasching* in Germany, *Martedi Grasso* in Italy, and *Fettisdagen* in Sweden.

Mardi Gras can take place anywhere from February 3 to March 9 in regular years, and from February 4 to March 9 in leap years.

Ash Wednesday

Ash Wednesday, the day after Shrove Tuesday, begins the season of Lent, a period of prayer and self-denial commemorating the 40 days Jesus spent fasting in the desert, can begin any day between February 4 and March 10 in common years, and as late as March 11 in leap years. The exact beginning of Lent is calculated differently by different Christian denominations.

Sheet music for the "Mardi Gras Rag," 1914

Saint Days

Each day in the year is considered a feast day for one or more saints. They are somewhat different in western Christianity (Catholicism and many forms of Protestantism) and in eastern (Orthodox) Christianity. There are many others; this is a selection.

In *Western Christianity*, February 4 is the feast day of Saints Andrew Corsini, Gilbert of Sempringham, John de Brito, Rabanus Maurus, Rimbert, and Veronica.

In *Eastern Orthodox Christianity*, it is also the commemoration of Saints Evagrius, Aventinus, Vincent of Troyes, Modan, Liephard, Vulgis, and Nithard. (These saints are honored on January 22 by "Old Calendrists.")

Honorary Months

Presidents, Congresses, and nations around the world issue proclamations recognizing particular months to honor certain causes. These events generally fall in February, though honorary months do come and go. Holidays established by states and nonprofit organizations are listed if verified. If not otherwise specified, all months are US. There is some variation from year to year; some celebratory months get added and others get dropped. Two places to get up to date information are the current edition of *Chase's Calendar of Events* or the website Brownielocks. Here are some honorary designations for February.

Black History Month (United States, Canada)

One of the most famous honorary months is Black History Month (sometimes African-American History Month). During Black History Month, important people and events in the African diaspora are commemorated. In the US and Canada, Black History Month is observed in February; in the UK, it's October.

"The First Vote," by Alfred Waud (1867)

Other honorary month designations for February include:

- American Heart Month
- Grapefruit Month
- International Month of Black Women in the Arts
- International Prenatal Infection Prevention Month
- LGBT History Month (United Kingdom)
- Library Lovers Month
- Marijuana Awareness Month
- National Bird-Feeding Month
- National Cherry Month
- National Condom Month
- National Children's Dental Health Month
- National Haiku Writing Month
- Pet Dental Health Month
- Season for Nonviolence (January 30-April 4, worldwide)
- Spunky Old Broads Month
- Youth Leadership Month

Moveable and Multi-Day Events

Some events take place over a specific week or time period. Start and finish dates may vary from year to year. Some events occur on different days each year (such as "fourth Saturday of a month"). These events sometimes take place on February 4.

First Week (begins January 29-February 4)

- Doppleganger Week (change your profile picture to someone else)
- Snow Sculpting Week (US)
- Women's Heart Week
- World Interfaith Harmony Week
- Children's Authors and Illustrators Week (first full week)

First Saturday (February 1-7)

- Ice Cream for Breakfast Day
- Take Your Child to the Library Day

First Sunday (February 1-7)

- Mother's Day (Kosovo)
- Super Bowl (US)

Just for Fun

Anybody can make up a holiday, and many people do! While none of these are officially recognized and some may come and go, here are a few more holidays for February 4.

- Liberace Day
- Quacker Day
- USO Day

Quote of the Day

"The most serious charge which can be brought against New England is not Puritanism but February."

Joseph Wood Krutch, critic, in *The Twelve Seasons* (1949)

About
the
Month
of

February

"February," from the *Brevarium Grimani* by Simon Bening (c.1510)

February: The Second Month

The February sunshine steeps your boughs
And tints the buds and swells the leaves within.

> — *William Cullen Bryant, "Among the Trees"*

The month of February takes its name from the Latin word *februum*, meaning purification, because the traditional Roman festival Februa, involving ritual purification, took place in what we now know as mid-February each year.

Because the Romans considered winter to be a monthless period, neither January nor February existed in the Roman calendar until 713 BCE, and when February did become a month, it was the last month of the year!

The number of days in February also varied in ancient times because the calendar had to be periodically adjusted to stay in line with the seasons. In some years, it was only 23 days long. When the calendar and the seasons got too far out of alignment, the Romans added a bonus month, called Intercalaris, consisting of 27 days, to bring everything back on track.

Our modern month of February begins with the calendar reforms of Julius Caesar, known as the Julian[†] calendar. February became 28 days long, with an extra "leap day" added every four years.

[†] For an explanation of calendar types, see "What Day of the Week is February 4?"

Although the Julian calendar remained stable for a long time, it wasn't perfectly accurate, and the calendar gradually drifted away from the seasons again.

In 1582, under Pope Gregory XIII, the Julian calendar gave way to the Gregorian calendar, still in use today. One of the Gregorian reforms was to eliminate Leap Year when a new century was not divisible by four. As a result, 1800 and 1900 were leap years, but 2000 was not.

Although the pronunciation "feb-roo-err-ee" is preferred, the common pronunciation "feb-ew-err-ee" (as if the month was spelled "Feb-u-ary") is acceptable as well.

From the point of view of meteorologists, February is the third month of winter in the northern hemisphere and the third month of summer in the southern hemisphere.

February always starts on the same day of the week as March and November in common years, and on the same day as August in leap years. It ends on the same weekday as October in all years, and in common years also ends on the same weekday as January. In leap years, February is the only month that ends on the same day of the week as it began.

Because February is the only month with 28 days in common years, it is the only month that can pass without a single full moon. This happened in 1999 and will happen again in 2018. It is also the only month (in common years) that can have exactly four full 7-day weeks. This happens once every six years and twice every eleven years.

"February," by Joachim von Sandrart

February in Other Cultures

The month of February has different names in different languages. Some nations use calendars other than the Gregorian, and their months may overlap with February. In lunar-based calendars, such as the Islamic calendar, months move through the seasons. Still, many languages often have a word for February itself.

Albanian: Shkurt
Anglo-Saxon: Sol-monath (cake month)
Arabic (Egypt, Sudan, Yemen): يونأغينافبراير (fibrāyir)
Arabic (Levant): حزيركانوشباط (shubāṭ)
Arabic (Libya): الصهناالنوار (an-nuwwār)
Arabic (Algeria and Tunisia): جأيفيفري (Fīfrī)
Arabic (Morocco): غينافبراير (fibrāyər)
Azerbaijani: Fevral
Basque: Otsail
Bulgarian: февруари (fevruari)
Chinese: 二月 (Cantonese: yihyuht; Mandarin: èryuè; Taiwanese: ji-goeh)
Corsican: Ferraghju
Croatian: Veljačaj
Czech: únor (month of submerging)
Finnish: Helmikuu (month of the pearl)
French: Février
German/Danish/Norwegian/Slovenian: Februar
Greek: Φεβρουάριος (Februários)
Haitian Creole: Fevriye

Hebrew: ינפברואר (febrû'ar)
Hindi: फ़रवरी (farvarī)
Hungarian: Február
Irish (Gaelic): Feabhra mí Feabhra
Italian: Febbraio
Japanese (traditional calendar): 二月 (nigatsu); 如月(kisaragi)
Kazakh: Ақпан (Aķpan)
Korean: 이월 (iweol)
Lithuanian: Vasaris
Maori: Hui tanguru
Old English: Solmōnaþ (mud month); Kale-monath (cabbage month)
Polish: Luty (month of ice)
Portuguese: Fevereiro
Russian: февраль (fevrali)
Scottish Gaelic: an Gearran
Sesotho: Hlakola
Spanish: Febrero
Swahili/Dutch/Swedish: Februari
Swazi: iNdlovana
Thai: Kumphaphan
Turkish: şubat
Ukrainian: лютий (ljutyj) (month of hard frost)
Vietnamese: 𣎃𠄩 (tháng ha)
Walloon: Fevrî
Welsh: Chwefror
Yiddish: פעברואַר (februar)
Zulu: uFebruwari

February Sayings and Superstitions

Here are some sayings and superstitions associated with the month of February.

February Weather Superstitions

February 12 to 14 were said to be "borrowed" from January. If those days were stormy, the year would have good weather, but if they were clear, the rest of the year would be foul.

When the cat lies in the sun in February / She will creep behind the stove in March.

Of all the months of the year / Curse a fair February.

If it thunders in February, it will frost in April.

If February give much snow / A fine summer it doth foreshow

February Wedding Superstitions

A February bride will be an affectionate wife / And a tender mother.

Married in February's sleepy weather / Life you'll tread in time together.

When February birds do mate / You wed nor dread your fate.

In Morocco, there is a ban on marriage during the seven days of *hesoum* (February 24 to March 4)

Valentine's Day Superstitions

The first man an unmarried woman sees on February 14 will be her future husband.

On Valentine's Day, if a girl writes all the names of her suitors on paper, wraps them in clay, and puts them in water, the piece that rises to the top first is the name of her husband to be.

If a woman sees a robin flying overhead on Valentine's Day, she will marry a sailor. If she sees a sparrow, she will marry a poor man but be very happy. If she sees a goldfinch, she will marry a rich person (happiness not guaranteed).

Leap Year Superstitions

Traditionally, women can propose to men on leap days, because the day had no legal status and therefor traditions did not apply. At one time, there was a Scottish law forbidding a man to refuse such a proposal. To ensure success, women should wear a red petticoat under their dress—and make sure it's partially visible to the man when they propose.

In some European countries, if a man refuses a woman's proposal on February 29, he must buy her 12 pairs of gloves.

In Scotland, it's considered unlucky to be born on a Leap Year's Day. Greeks consider it unlucky to be married during a leap year, and especially on a leap day. If you divorce during a leap year, you will never find happiness again.

February Symbols

Birthstone: Amethyst, representing piety, humility, spiritual wisdom, and sincerity

Birth Flowers: Violet and Primrose

Soviet postage stamp of an amethyst from the 1963 "Precious Stone of the Urals" series

Violet (Photo: Andrew Bossi CC BY-SA 2.5)

Still life (primroses, pears, and pomegranates),
by Henri Fantin-Latour

"February," by Eugène Grasset

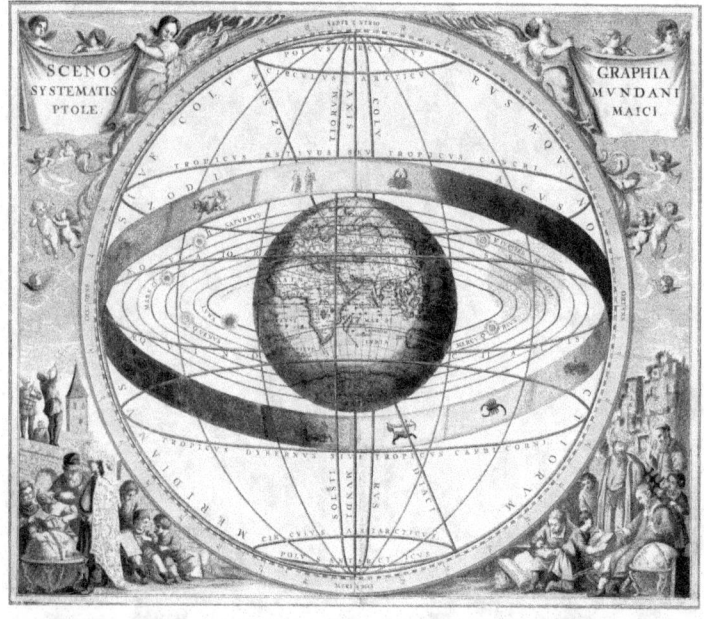

Scenography of the Ptolemaic Cosmography, by Johannes van Loon, based on Andreas Cellarius's *Harmonia Macrocosmica,* 1660

February 4 Zodiac Signs

From the perspective of someone on Earth, the Sun appears to move through the sky throughout the year, along a path astronomers call the *ecliptic plane*. The ecliptic plane is divided into twelve constellations, known as the zodiac, based on traditionally observed patterns of stars. On your birthday, you can't see your constellation, because it's in the daytime sky.

The zodiac was first developed by Babylonian astronomers about 2,500 years ago. Because they were unaware that the Earth wobbles like a spinning top (known as *precession*), they didn't make allowance for the fact that the Sun's path through the zodiac changes over time.

That means there are now two sets of dates for your birth sign. The *tropical dates* are the original Babylonian dates; the *sidereal dates* tell you where the Sun actually appears as it moves along its annual path.

For February 4, the tropical sign is **Aquarius** and the sidereal sign is **Capricorn.**

Aquarius

Tropical January 20 to February 19
Sidereal February 12 to March 8 (March 9 in leap years)

Aquarius is one of the oldest recognized constellations, originally representing the Babylonian god Ea. In Latin, Aquarius means "water-carrier," represented in its symbol. In Greek mythology, Aquarius is sometimes associated with Deucalion, who survived a world-cleansing flood. In Chinese astronomy, it is known as the Black Tortoise of the North (北方玄武, Běi Fāng Xuán Wǔ).

In astrology, Aquarius is considered to be masculine and extroverted, and despite the name is an air sign. Aquarians are supposed to be philanthropical, inventive, and individualistic.

Capricorn

Tropical December 22 to January 20
Sidereal January 15 to February 14

The origins of the constellation Capricorn date back to Sumeria and Babylonia. Based on Enki, the Sumerian god of wisdom and waters, Capricorn has the head and upper body of a mountain goat and the lower body and tail of a fish. The mountain goat represents ambition and intelligence, the fish represents passion and spirituality.

An earth sign, Capricorn is ruled by the planet Saturn. They are often thought to be responsible, patient, ambitious and loyal, but can sometimes be seen as conceited, distrusting, and unimaginative. Capricornians are supposed to be compatible with Taurus, Pisces, and Virgo, but not with Aries, Sagittarius, or Leo.

Illustration by Edward Penfield

What Day of the Week is February 4?

On what day of the week does February 4 fall?

Surprisingly, this isn't an easy question. Because the calendar year is 365 days long (366 in leap years), it doesn't divide evenly by the seven days of the week.

Also, the Earth goes around the Sun in about 365-1/4 days, so a calendar tends to drift over time. That's why the same date falls on different weekdays in different years.

This is made even more complicated by a change in calendars that took place in 1582. Our modern calendar has its roots in ancient Rome, in a calendar reform conducted by Julius Caesar. Caesar commissioned mathematicians to attack the problem, and they came up with the idea of leap years, and thus standardized the calendar for centuries to come. This was called the Julian calendar.

Over time, however, the small errors in Caesar's calculation compounded. That's why Pope Gregory XIII commissioned the Gregorian calendar, used in most of the world today. Some countries converted in 1582, when the calendar was first developed; some converted later; other still haven't changed.

Gregorian and Julian aren't the only types of calendars. The Hebrew year, the Islamic year, and many other calendars are used in different parts of the world and among different people.

You can convert Gregorian dates to other calendars, including the Hebrew calendar, the Islamic calendar, and even the Mayan calendar by visiting the Fourmilab Calendar Converter at http://www.fourmilab.ch/documents/calendar/.

Chinese calendar systems are quite complex and have changed several times; a full discussion is far beyond the scope of this book. If you're interested, you can find information here: http://www.hermetic.ch/cal_stud/chinese_cal.htm.

On Names and Dates

Historians use "CE" (Common Era) and "BCE" (Before the Common Era) instead of the more common "AD" (Anno Domini, or Year of Our Lord) and "BC" (Before Christ), reflecting the fact that the year-numbering system established by the Gregorian calendar is used throughout the world in many countries not culturally Christian.

The CE/BCE designation dates back to at least 1708, and has been adopted as a standard by the United Nations and the Universal Postal Union. Because this series of books covers events and people of all nations and cultures, we use the CE/BCE terms.

The abbreviation "O.S." ("Old Style") and "N.S." ("New Style") on some dates refers to the fact that the Russian Empire (in particular) did not switch from the Julian to the Gregorian calendar at the same time as the rest of Europe, and therefore some figures and events have two dates.

Also, in the Julian calendar in England in the 16th century, the year began on March 25 rather than January 1. To avoid confusion with Gregorian dates, dates between January and March were often written using both years.

People and events whose original names are not in the Western alphabet have their native names (where possible) in the appropriate script shown in parenthesis. If you are using an e-reader to access an electronic version of this book, all characters don't always display on all devices.

A 50-year brass perpetual calendar.

Quote of the Day

"Time is an illusion, lunchtime doubly so."

Douglas Adams,
from *The Hitchhiker's Guide to the Galaxy*

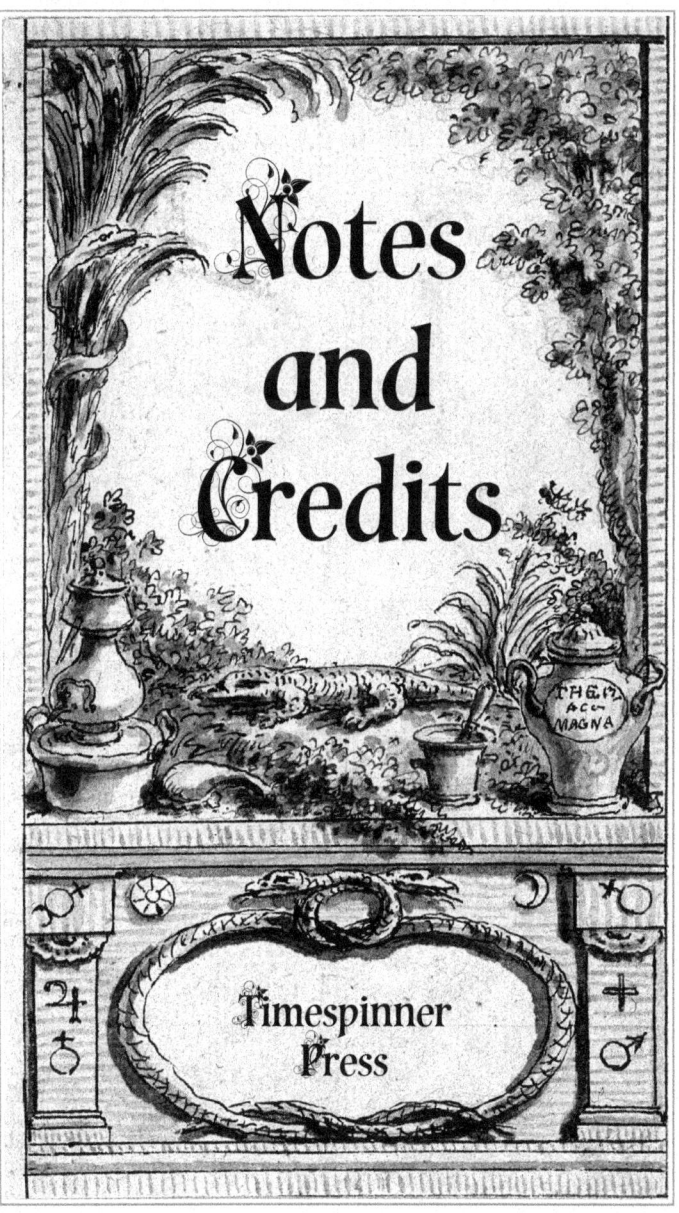

Notes
and
Credits

THER
ACU
MAGNA

Timespinner
Press

Cartoon by John T. McCutcheon

Copyright, Credit, and Contact

Follow Us

Our blog "This Day in History" (http://
timespinnerpress.com/this-day-in-history/) features short
articles on events and people associated with each day, and
updates several times each week. Also subscribe to the
"Quote of the Day" at http://timespinnerpress.com/quote-
of-the-day/. You can get daily links by following us on
Facebook at TimespinnerPress, or on Twitter as
@sidewisethinker.

Contact Us

Find an error or a format problem? Want information about
the series, about us, or about when the volume for your
special day might be available? Please email us at
editor@timespinnerpress.com. (We also take requests if your
special day isn't yet complete. Please give us at least six
weeks' notice if possible.)

Sources

We owe a great debt to Wikipedia, which is our first stop for
research. We attempt to make independent confirmation of
all important dates and facts through a variety of other
sources.

Other sources we frequently use include the Library of
Congress; "on this day" listings from *Encyclopedia Britannica*,
the *New York Times*, and the BBC; Omniglot for the names of
months in other languages; *Chase's Calendar of Events*; and, of
course, the always essential Google.

All art and photographs are either in the public domain, used under a Creative Commons license, or with a "fair use" justification, and most frequently come from Wikimedia Commons and the Library of Congress Prints and Photographs Division.

Attribution is provided where possible, or as requested by the copyright owner, or when there is particular historical significance, listed below. For information about any particular illustration or photograph, please contact us.

Credits

1. TThe cover painting of George Washington was created by Thomas Sully in 1820, and is from the Lyndon B. Johnson Museum Collection, US National Archives (ID 192421). It is in the public domain because its copyright has expired.

2. The illustration of the month of February used on the back cover is from the French Gothic illuminated manuscript *Les Très Riches Heures du duc de Berry* by the Limbourg Brothers, Jean Colombe, and an intermediate painter whose name is lost to history. It is in the public domain because its copyright has expired.

3. The box graphic used on the first page is from a 1916 pamphlet entitled "Divorce versus Democracy" authored by G. K. Chesterton, originally published in London by the Society of St. Peter and St. Paul. It is in the public domain in the US because it was published prior to 1923, and is in the public domain in all countries (including the country of origin) in which the copyright time is the author's life plus 70 years or less.

4. The graphic design for the section pages in this book is from a design originally created for a pharmacy label. It is courtesy of Wellcome Images (ICV No 11073, photo V0010813), and is used here under CC BY-SA 4.0.

5. The illustration of George Washington's presidential inauguration is from the book *United States: A History*, by John Clark Ridpath, published by the US History

Corporation, Boston, in 1893. It is in the public domain because its copyright has expired. The artist is unknown.

6. The 2015 photograph of the Mount Rushmore sculpture of George Washington was taken by "Purple Bullet," who released the photograph into the public domain without restriction.

7. The image from the 1941 film *The 47 Ronin*, directed by Kenji Mizoguchi, is in the public domain according to a 2006 Japanese court ruling that all films produced in Japan prior to 1953 were now in the public domain.

8. The photograph from the Yalta Conference is courtesy of the National Museum of the US Navy. It is in the public domain because it is a work prepared by an officer or employee of the US government as part of that person's official duties. The image has been cropped.

9. The 1927 photograph of Charles Lindbergh is courtesy of the Library of Congress (digital ID cph.3a23920). It is in the public domain because it was published in the United States between 1923 and 1963, and although the image was originally copyrighted, according to the Library, the copyright was not renewed.

10. The photograph of Wanda Rutkiewicz is in the public domain under Article 3 of the copyright law of March 29, 1926, of the Republic of Poland and Article 2 of the copyright law of July 10, 1952, of the People's Republic of Poland because it was first published without a clear copyright notice prior to May 23, 1994. The photographer is unknown.

11. The 2016 photograph of Alice Cooper is by "Biha," and was taken with the support of Wikimedia Deutchland as part of the "Festival Summer" project. It is used here under CC BY-SA 4.0.

12. The poster for a 2006 Clint Black concert at the Chumash Casino Resort, Santa Ynez, California, is by Dwight McCann (www.dwightmccann.com) and is used here under CC BY-SA 2.5.

13. The publicity photograph of Ida Lupino is in the public domain because it was first published in the United States between 1923 and 1977 without a copyright notice.

Traditionally, publicity photographs are not copyrighted because of the way in which they are intended to be used.

14. The photograph of Clyde Tombaugh appeared in the June 1930 issue of *Popular Science Monthly*. Although there was a copyright notice, the copyright was not renewed, and as the work was published in the US between 1923 and 1963, the copyright has expired.

15. The 1951 photograph of Lisa Fonssagrives in Paddington Station, London, was taken by Toni Frissell, and was originally published in Harper's Bazaar magazine. It is part of the Toni Frissell collection at the Library of Congress (digital ID cph.3g04320), and under the terms of the Instrument of Gift, it has been released into the public domain.

16. The illustration by Patrick Nagel is presumed to be copyrighted and is not in the public domain. Its use here is under "fair use" provisions of the copyright code. It is used to illustrate a biographical entry for the artist, no free equivalent is available, it is printed in black & white instead of color, and the size and resolution are insufficient to support the creation of counterfeit goods.

17. The crew photograph from the Apollo 14 mission is in the public domain because it was solely created by NASA.

18. The 1968 photograph of Liberace was taken by Allan Warren, and is used here under CC BY-SA 3.0.

19. The 1866 painting "February in the Isle of Wight" by John Brett is in the public domain because its copyright has expired. The image is courtesy Google Art Project; the original can be found in the Birmingham Museum and Art Gallery.

20. The 1955 photograph of Rosa Parks with Dr. Martin Luther King, Jr., was originally published in *Ebony* magazine. It was taken on behalf of the United States Information Agency and is available from the US National Archives (ID 306-PDS-65-1882, Box 93). It is in the public domain as a work created by an employee of the US government as part of that person's official duties.

21. The sheet music cover for the 1914 song "Mardi Gras Rag", by Lyons and Yosco, was published by Geo. W. Meyer Music

Co., New York. It is in the public domain because it was first published prior to January 1, 1923.

22. The illustration "The First Vote" by Alfred R. Waud originally appeared on the cover of *Harper's* magazine in 1867. It is in the public domain because its copyright has expired.

23. The 1860 illustration "The Curlers," by Roger Griffith, is in the public domain because its copyright has expired.

24. The painting "February" is from the *Brevarium Grimani*, circa 1510, and is in the public domain because its copyright has expired.

25. The painting "February" by Joachim von Sandrart is in the public domain because its copyright has expired. The original can be found in the Staatsgalerie im Neuen Schloss, Schleißheim, Germany.

26. The 1815 woodcut of a proposal is in the public domain because its copyright has expired.

27. The 1896 drawing "February" by Eugène Grasset is in the public domain because its copyright has expired.

28. The 1963 Soviet postage stamp of an amethyst from the "Precious Stones of the Urals" series is not an object of copyright according to article 1259 of Book IV of the Civil Code of the Russian Federation No. 230-FZ, 12/18/2006.

29. The photograph of violets at the Abbey Church of Saint Peter, Salzburg, Austria, was taken by Andrew Bossi and used here under CC BY-SA 2.5.

30. The painting "*Nature morte (primevères, poires et grenades)*" by Henri Fantin-Latour is in the public domain because its copyright has expired. The original can be found at the Kröller-Müller Museum, Otterlo, Netherlands. Image courtesy Google Art Project by way of Wikimedia Commons.

31. The celestial sphere is from *Scenography of the Ptolemaic Cosmography*, by Johannes van Loon, based on Andreas Cellarius's *Harmonia Macrocosmica*, 1660. It is in the public domain because its copyright has expired.

32. The 1906 automobile calendar is by Edward Penfield, and is in the collection of the Library of Congress Prints and Photographs Division. It is in the public domain because its copyright has expired.

33. The 50-year perpetual calendar photograph is in the public domain.

34. The cartoon by John T. McCutcheon is from his 1905 collection *The Mysterious Stranger and Other Cartoons by John T. McCutcheon.* It is in the public domain because its copyright has expired.

License Description and Terms

Aside from material purely in the public domain, photographs and other material in this book are used under specific licenses permitting free use, usually with an attribution requirement. For full text and terms of these licenses, click or enter the appropriate links below. If you believe there is an error in the copyright status or attribution of any of these images, please email us.

- Creative Commons Attribution 2.0 Generic (CC-BY 2.0): http://creativecommons.org/licenses/by/2.0/deed.en
- Creative Commons Attribution-Share Alike 3.0 Generic (CC-BY-SA 3.0): http://creativecommons.org/licenses/by-sa/3.0/
- Creative Commons Attribution-Share Alike 2.5 Generic (CC-BY-SA 2.5): http://creativecommons.org/licenses/by-sa/2.5/deed.en
- Creative Commons Attribution-Share Alike 2.0 Generic (CC-BY-SA 2.0): http://creativecommons.org/licenses/by/2.0/deed.en
- Creative Commons Attribution-Share Alike 1.0 Generic (CC-BY-SA 1.0): http://creativecommons.org/licenses/by-sa/1.0/deed.en
- CC0 1.0 Universal (CC0 1.0) Public Domain Dedication (CC0 1.0) http://creativecommons.org/publicdomain/zero/1.0/deed.en
- GNU Free Documentation License (GFDL): http://en.wikipedia.org/wiki/Wikipedia:Text_of_the_GNU_Free_Documentation_License
- License Art Libre (Free Art License): http://artlibre.org

Other Books from Timespinner Press

The Story of a Special Day
Michael Dobson

A series of (eventually) 366 volumes covering everything that happened on your special day! Events, births, deaths, quotes, holidays, and much more. It's like a birthday card they'll never throw away!

US$7.95 print / US$2.99 ebook.

From Plassey to Pakistan
Humayun Mirza

The history of British Colonial India and the formation of Pakistan from the unique perspective of the son of Pakistan's first president and last of the royal line of Bengal, Bihar, and Orissa! This unique historical document tells the inside story of this distinguished family, including the detailed story of the coup that toppled his father from power!

US$27.95 print

Michael Dobson

A Whole New Navy: America's War in the Pacific

Miles Durr

The most comprehensive and detailed description of America's naval war in the Pacific ever—every battle, every ship, every task force and every task group from Pearl Harbor through the Japanese surrender! A must-have for the collection of every World War II buff!

US$29.95 print

Improbable History: The Weird, the Obscure, and the Strangely Important

edited by Michael Dobson

From the birth of Western civilization to the rescue of Apollo 13, from the Leaning Tower of Pisa to Florence's Duomo, history has often turned on small, improbable details. Whatever happened to the ancient Samaritan people? Why did a fortuitous rainstorm allow the British to conquer India? How did an air raid in Italy lead to the development of chemotherapy? What happened when Albert Einstein met Adolf Hitler on the streets of Berlin? How did the Japanese manage to attack the US mainland using balloons? A cast of award-winning writers tackle some of the strangest tales in history!

US$19.95 print